BREAKING THE LOOPS

I'm not Enough

Marnie Sole

652 Hogans Rd North Tumbulgum NSW 2490.
www.contempopublishing.com

A catalogue entry for this book is available from the National Library of Australia.

ISBN (Paperback): 978 1 7645975 0 0

Cover design by Rubi Creations Digital.
Internal design by Contempo Publishing.

Printed and distributed internationally by Ingram Spark.

First published in 2026 by Contempo Publishing.

Disclaimer

This book weaves together personal reflection, lived experience, and illustrative storytelling in service of awareness and insight. While grounded in real emotional truths, the stories shared are **composites** drawn from multiple experiences across time. Names, identifying details, and certain circumstances have been altered to ensure the privacy of individuals. Some characters represent blended experiences rather than any one person. Any resemblance to actual individuals, living or deceased, is therefore coincidental.

The reflections, prompts, and practices offered throughout this book are intended as invitations into self-inquiry, not prescriptions or guarantees of specific outcomes. Growth, healing, and change are deeply individual processes. Engaging with these reflections does not ensure particular results, nor does it replace professional psychological, medical, or therapeutic support.

This book does not claim to diagnose, treat, or cure any condition. If you are experiencing significant distress, trauma, or mental health challenges, you are encouraged to seek support from a qualified professional. You remain responsible for how you choose to interpret and apply the ideas presented here.

By reading this book, you acknowledge that your journey is your own — and that this work is a companion, not a promise.

Dedication

To my parents, my family, my friends, my lovers and partners, and every soul who crossed my path—for the tenderness and the ache.

Thank you for the moments that sent me into the depths, cracking old stories open and revealing the truth beneath the noise: the woman I always was.

A special thank you to Tiff, Nik, Sammy, Coral, Robii, and Shazzy—for seeing this work from different worlds and helping it land more fully in this one.

For the academic lens, the lived response, the marketing clarity, the structural wisdom, the tech magic, the fifth-dimensional conversations, and the grounded questions that made it clearer, sharper, and more human.

This book is stronger because each of you met it with your own eyes.

About the Author

Marnie Sole is a behaviour consultant, university lecturer and author, whose work bridges behavioural science, quantum physics and timeless principles of consciousness. For more than three decades, she has worked with individuals, educators and small groups, helping people uncover the unconscious beliefs that shape their lives and guiding them to rewrite those patterns with awareness and authenticity.

She's worked within the education system, designing individual behaviour support plans and guiding teachers to understand the unseen forces shaping human response. Over time, she recognised that every pattern of behaviour originates from a deeper story, a subconscious program born from early emotional experiences and core wounds of worth, safety and belonging.

In her signature *Breaking the Loops* series, Marnie explores how those subconscious beliefs generate thoughts and feelings that drive behaviour, which in turn produce the repeating outcomes we experience as 'life'. She explains that each thought-feeling-behaviour sequence vibrates at a measurable frequency, sending a signal into the quantum field and drawing back matching experiences. This cycle – known to both modern science and ancient consciousness traditions – is the feedback loop through which we continually recreate our reality.

Marnie's work shows readers how to interrupt that loop through awareness rather than force. By identifying the emotional programs running beneath everyday reactions, people can dissolve the energy of the wound itself—not by rejecting the past, but by meeting it with understanding. When thought, emotion, and behaviour come into coherence, the frequency emitted into the field changes, and so does what life reflects back.

Her voice is accessible and grounded, weaving the clarity of behavioural analysis with the insight of quantum mechanics and the compassion found in timeless spiritual psychology. She calls this fusion 'frequency architecture' – the deliberate design of inner alignment that reorganises outer experience.

Marnie's mission is to guide others to become the architects of their own reality. Whether speaking to educators, mentoring individuals or writing for a broad audience, she offers a bridge between the measurable and the mystical, between data and devotion. Her voice is not that of a guru, but of a companion on the climb—practical, articulate and profoundly human.

Through *Breaking the Loops*, Marnie Sole invites readers to see that nothing in their story is wasted. Every wound carries information, every belief can be rewritten, and every emotion is energy in motion seeking coherence. When we understand the patterns that once kept us safe, we reclaim the freedom to create from truth rather than trauma.

Marnie lives in northern New South Wales, Australia, where she balances her professional consultancy with writing, teaching and time in nature. Her work continues to evolve around a single guiding question: *What becomes possible when we live as the frequency of our own wisdom?*

If you recognise yourself in these pages, there's more waiting for you. Go deeper at: www.marniesole.com

Contents

Key Terms: A Soul-Aligned Glossary

Throughout this book you'll notice language that blends neuroscience, behavioural psychology, quantum science and spiritual insight. These ideas are not abstract theories. They describe real patterns that shape how we think, feel and act.

As you move through the chapters, these terms will become part of a new vocabulary for understanding your inner world. Rather than memorising definitions, allow them to deepen through reflection and lived experience.

Core Wounds

Core wounds are the deep emotional imprints formed during early life experiences where our needs for love, safety, belonging or worth were not fully met.

These moments shape the way we interpret ourselves and the world. Over time they crystallise into beliefs such as *I am not enough*, *I am unlovable*, or *I must prove my worth.*

Core wounds are not personal failures. They are adaptive responses formed by a young nervous system trying to make sense of difficult experiences.

When left unconscious, these wounds quietly organise our relationships, choices and emotional reactions throughout life.

Core Beliefs

Core beliefs are the unconscious conclusions we form about ourselves because of our early experiences.

They become the invisible lens through which we interpret reality. From these beliefs arise our thoughts, emotions, expectations and behaviours.

Most people are not aware of their core beliefs because they operate below conscious awareness. Instead, we simply experience their effects through repeating life patterns.

When a core belief shifts, the patterns built around it begin to dissolve.

Conditioning, Patterns and Loops

Once a core belief forms, the mind begins organising experiences around it.

We develop familiar emotional reactions, behavioural strategies and relational dynamics that reinforce the belief. Over time these become **patterns**.

When these patterns repeat consistently across relationships and situations, they form what this book calls **loops**.

A loop is a self-reinforcing cycle where beliefs create behaviours, behaviours create outcomes, and those outcomes strengthen the original belief.

Breaking the loop begins by becoming conscious of the pattern.

Frequency

Frequency refers to the energetic tone created by our thoughts, emotions and beliefs.

In physics, everything in the universe exists as vibrating energy. In human experience, our emotional states also carry distinct energetic signatures.

Emotions such as shame, fear and resentment tend to contract the nervous system and narrow our perception. Emotions like love, peace and gratitude expand our awareness and openness.

The emotional frequency we live in most often shapes the quality of our experiences and the choices available to us.

Alignment

Alignment is the experience of living in coherence with your authentic self.

When you are aligned, your thoughts, emotions, values and actions move in the same direction. You are no longer acting from unconscious conditioning or the need to prove your worth.

Alignment often feels like clarity in the mind, calm in the nervous system and a quiet sense of inner truth guiding your decisions.

Core Wounds

Early emotional pain

Core Beliefs

Unconscious beliefs

Patterns & Loops

Repeating behaviors

Emotional Frequency

Energy state

Reality Experience

Life as we perceive it

Quantum Science

Quantum science studies the behaviour of matter and energy at the smallest measurable levels of reality.

One of its key discoveries is that particles do not behave like fixed objects. Instead, they exist as fields of possibility that are influenced by interaction and observation.

While quantum physics is a complex scientific field, it offers a powerful metaphor for personal transformation: reality is not as fixed or predetermined as it appears.

Our awareness, attention and emotional state influence the way we experience the world around us.

Quantum Field

The quantum field refers to the invisible field of energy and information that underlies physical reality.

Rather than seeing the universe as separate objects interacting, modern physics increasingly describes reality as interconnected fields of energy.

In practical terms, this means we are not isolated individuals acting in a disconnected world. We are participants within a larger field of relationship and possibility.

Our thoughts, emotions and beliefs act like signals that interact with this field. The patterns we hold internally influence the experiences that emerge externally.

Portal

A portal is a moment of heightened awareness created through challenge, discomfort or emotional intensity.

Although these moments can feel painful, they often mark the threshold of transformation. When we move through them consciously rather than avoiding them, they become openings into deeper understanding and growth.

In this way, the wound itself becomes the doorway to wisdom.

Breaking the Loops

Understanding the Journey

We all carry wounds—some visible, most invisible. They often begin in childhood, shaped by family dynamics, school systems, early relationships or moments where our authentic self was misunderstood, rejected or not fully seen. These formative experiences birth what we call core wounds—deep-seated beliefs about who we are and what we're worth. These core wounds become the unconscious stories that run our lives. They become the lens through which we interpret events, the script we use to make sense of the world and the emotional signals we send into the quantum field. Psychology and neuroscience show that a large portion of our behaviour is driven by unconscious patterns and automatic processes – the beliefs and emotional imprints formed early in life that quietly shape how we think, feel and respond. In every moment, we are broadcasting a frequency – a unique blend of our most dominant thoughts, beliefs and emotional states. According to the principles of quantum physics, everything in the universe is made of energy, including us. Our internal state radiates outward and interacts with the quantum field—a sea of potentiality that responds to vibration, not just words. This means we are constantly in a 'co-creative' dance with life. If we carry a wound like 'I'm not good enough', that frequency draws to us situations, people and outcomes that either reinforce or challenge that belief. This is not about blame. It's about power. The universe is not punishing us – it is mirroring us – offering repeated opportunities to notice, to heal and to choose again.

To change our lives by breaking our loops, we must first change our inner world. This begins with self-awareness. Our core wounds are often programmed into the subconscious mind early in life, much like code running quietly in the background of a computer system – shaping our thoughts, emotions and behaviours without our conscious consent. These wounded patterns operate on autopilot – looping – until we bring them into the light of conscious awareness.

When we shine awareness on the beliefs and emotional imprints we've absorbed (often unquestioned since childhood), we reclaim the power to rewrite the code. But awareness alone is not enough. We must 'feel into' the origins of these wounds. When you go inward and meet those feelings, do so with compassion. Create a sacred space of non-judgment. Become the loving witness for your inner child. Let yourself feel the grief, the rage, the abandonment, the shame – whatever arises.

Don't avoid the pain by jumping straight into pleasure or distraction. That only perpetuates the loop. Pain must be acknowledged before it can be transmuted. Whether it's alcohol, sex, shopping, workaholism, food, drugs, scrolling or even excessive positivity—we each have our own escape routes.

Instead, confront the pain head-on. Witness the fear, the lack, the rejection, the loss. Hold space for it with tenderness, curiosity and empathy.

When you offer forgiveness to yourself, to others, to life itself – you begin to dissolve the emotional charge. And in that sacred act, you deprogram the old pattern and make room for a new frequency: one based on truth, love and self-honouring.

Self-awareness is the portal. Feeling is the path. Forgiveness is the key, and from there, reprogramming becomes not just possible, but inevitable. This is how we shift our vibration and begin to author a new reality—one rooted not in old wounds, but in our new wholeness.

The Breaking the Loops series was created as a companion on your journey of self-discovery and empowerment. Each book will explore a different core wound, guiding you to:

- Discover how it formed
- Identify how that wound shows up in your thoughts, emotions, behaviors, and relationships
- Recognise how it sends a particular frequency into the quantum field
- Learn practical tools both scientifically validated and spiritually grounded to shift the internal story

- Raise your emotional and energetic frequency so that you begin to magnetise experiences from your truth rather than your trauma.

This is not a process of fixing yourself—you are not broken. It is a process of becoming aware, choosing again and allowing your innate wisdom and wholeness to rise.

This series is born from the integration of neuroscience, psychology, spirituality and quantum science. It is grounded in lived experience and inspired by the transformative work of those who have shaped the landscape of human healing and consciousness, including Dr Joe Dispenza's quantum neuroplasticity, John Bligh Nutting's core belief work, Pia Melody's trauma and relational frameworks, Dr David Hawkins' spiritual teachings and Map of Consciousness and Byron Katie's inquiry into thought and truth. Each offers a lens through which we can understand the self, unravel old loops of unworthiness and remember the freedom that has always been ours.

At the core of all this lies Quantum Science, which confirms what ancient wisdom has always taught: we are not just matter, we are energy. Our thoughts are signals, our emotions are frequencies, and the field around us is responsive to both. The quantum field reflects not what we want, but who we are being, what we believe, what we feel and what we energetically *broadcast*.

This body of work is about reclaiming your power as the conscious creator of your life – not by bypassing pain, but by understanding the science of transformation. By bringing awareness to core wounds, bringing the unconscious to consciousness, questioning the programs that no longer serve and choosing new thoughts and elevated emotional states, we begin to rewire the brain, recondition the body and shift our vibrational signature. We rewrite our story and break our loops.

Healing is not just about feeling better, it's about becoming energetically aligned with a new reality, and from that frequency, life meets us differently.

This series invites you to become a *Soul Alchemist* – to transmute your pain into power, your wounds into wisdom and your fear into freedom. The transformation begins with awareness, deepens with inquiry and becomes embodied through practice. As your frequency shifts, so does your life, because you're not just thinking new thoughts — you're being someone new. Each book is your mirror, your map, and your medicine.

Before You Skip Ahead and Skip the Work... Let's be honest.

There's a reason so many people read books like this and still don't change. They skip the work. Not because they don't want to heal, but because pausing to reflect, to write, to feel, can be uncomfortable. Even inconvenient.

Maybe you don't know what to write. Maybe you tell yourself you'll come back to it later. Maybe you just don't like what comes up when you sit in silence with yourself. But let me tell you something gently and truthfully:

Insight without action doesn't create change.

Reading isn't the same as healing.

This book isn't here to entertain your mind. It's here to help you shift your frequency, your patterns, your story. And the real shifts don't happen in the reading. They happen in the doing.

So, throughout these pages, you'll find invitations and prompts, journal cues, frequency mapping, opportunities for self-inquiry, breathwork and energy recalibrations.

These aren't optional extras. They are the access points. They are where transformation begins.

This isn't just a book to read. It's a space to meet yourself. You'll find pages here that are intentionally left open, not empty, but waiting. For your thoughts, your honesty, your patterns as they reveal themselves. You can write directly into these pages or use your own journal. What matters is that you don't just move past what lands... you stay with it long enough to respond.

If you're not willing to pause, pick up a pen and get honest with yourself, these words might resonate but they won't rewrite your story or break the looping.

So, here's your invitation:

Grab a pen.

Open your heart.

Breathe.

You don't have to do it perfectly. You just have to do it.

Let's begin – together.

Marnie's Story

Born to Hold It All Together

'The wound is the place where the Light enters you.'

— Rumi

I grew up an only child, but not truly. My father had left a woman and three children to be with my mother, and together they had me. So, while I have half-siblings, I was raised in solitude. My early years were nomadic – travelling Australia in an old S-series Valiant and caravan until I turned 6. It was a strange, beautiful kind of freedom, full of red dirt roads and the wide Australian sky, until it was time to 'settle down'. When school began, we anchored ourselves in the western suburbs of Sydney, but the stillness of suburbia only revealed what constant movement had masked: cracks in my family's foundation.

My parents in those early years were what you'd call happy drunks: the life of the party, laughing and dancing, drinks in hand, Johnny Cash on cassette…but the alcohol flowed constantly. Eventually, it took a toll. The good times began to fray, and they both ended up in Alcoholics Anonymous, a turning point, but not the end of the unravelling.

My father, 14 years older than my mother, was emotionally absent. He was there, technically, but not there; however, I've come to understand why. He was born in the 1930s, in the thick of the Great Depression, one of seven children, three of whom didn't survive. His father was a violent alcoholic, and there was often not enough food to go around. My dad left home early, not out of rebellion, but out of survival. He became a hard worker and a provider, a typical man of his generation, one who measured love in actions, not in words. Emotional connection wasn't modelled for him; tenderness wasn't safe. He didn't know how to connect, so he withdrew. That was the only emotional map he had.

Yet, there was another influence in his life, one that I now see shaped me in quieter, more magical ways. His mother Grace, my paternal grandmother, was a spiritualist. She ran spiritualist churches in Sydney and gave flower readings at Christmas. As a child, I remember being captivated by her. She'd speak about mystical realms, energy and spirit guides as if they were as real as the chair beneath you. Her presence seeded something in me – a sense that there was more to life than the visible, more to truth than what could be explained. That early exposure to the unseen offered a strange kind of grounding, a knowing that has always lived inside me.

While my father's absence hurt, I no longer see it as malice. I see it as unhealed pain. A pain he didn't know how to speak of, and likely never felt safe enough to face. He did what many men of that time did: he coped the only way he knew how – by shutting down, by soldiering on and disappearing.

My mother, by contrast, poured all her love into me. I was her world, but behind her love lived a haunting, the legacy of a deeply traumatic childhood. Her childhood was one of chaos and violence, raised by a mother who was a violent alcoholic, frequently placing her in harm's way with predatory men. Abuse was her inheritance. Her self-worth was fractured early, and she clung to my father, older and emotionally unavailable, like a lifeline. She had never known safety. Never known the kind of fatherly love that protects and uplifts. So, when she met my father – older and seemingly stable – she clung to the idea that he could be her anchor. But when that anchor broke, she unravelled and I became her everything.

She was diagnosed with severe anxiety and depression and eventually institutionalised. She had shock treatments and medicated silence. I now understand this through an adult lens, but back then I was a teenager hiding the truth from the world—living alone, pretending everything was fine. My father had abandoned me, and my mother's absence was a revolving door of crisis and return.

When she was home, I cared for her; when she wasn't, I managed my grandmother, the very same violent alcoholic who had terrorised my mother. She stabbed a man. She killed another. I was still a girl but already carrying the weight of three generations of trauma, trying to keep things calm, keep things safe and keep things together, because if I didn't, who would?

So, I learned to scan every room before I entered it. I became hyper-attuned to others' emotional states. I soothed. I fixed. I rescued. I stayed busy. I over-functioned. Not because I wanted to, but because on some level I believed that was the price of safety. That was the price of love. That was how I made sense of the chaos. That was how I survived.

In those teenage years, living alone while no one really knew what was going on, I found my own ways to cope. I smoked a lot of weed. I was high most days at school—not to rebel, but to escape. To numb. I failed my HSC and yet, somehow, I still got into university by excelling at the entrance exam. I studied to become a special education teacher – the child who held it all together, becoming the adult who would help others find their way.

This legacy is where my core beliefs were formed.

I am not enough — yet. But if I do more, maybe I will be.

Love is earned through sacrifice.

My value lies in what I can fix, soothe, or carry for others.

If I don't hold it together, everything will fall apart.

I share this story not from a lens of victimhood. I don't subscribe to victimhood. I believe that every experience in our lives, no matter how painful, is part of a divine unfolding. Each one is here to grow us, stretch us and initiate us into a deeper truth. Life doesn't happen to us – it happens *for* us – and the more we shine light on what we've lived through, the more we illuminate the wisdom it has given us.

These beliefs I carried didn't just live in my mind. They pulsed through my energy. They shaped my nervous system, my behaviour, my relationships and even the kinds of love I allowed myself to receive. They weren't just beliefs. They were frequencies – energetic signatures emitting shame, over-responsibility and fear, and, in turn, drawing in experiences that validated those very frequencies.

But that's the magic: when we become aware, we become free. When we uncover these distortions, we awaken the power to transmute them, and that's the heart of *Breaking the Loops*.

Maybe you, too, were taught to trade your authenticity for acceptance. Maybe you became the strong one, the responsible one, the peacekeeper—not because you wanted to, but because no one else knew how to be. Maybe your wound didn't form because something was wrong with you, but because you were too young to carry so much, and yet you did.

This book is for that part of you, the one who silently wonders, 'Why do I keep repeating this pattern?'. The one who's tired of trying to earn worthiness through over giving, disappearing and people pleasing. The one who knows there's more – more truth, more freedom, more joy – but can't quite reach it.

Healing doesn't mean erasing your past. It means reclaiming the self that existed before the wound, before the beliefs, before the masks. When the programming becomes obsolete and needs *deleting.* When we make the unconscious, conscious.

As you'll discover in the chapters ahead, our wounds – when understood – become invitations, and the 'not *enough-ness*' we've carried isn't truth. It's a distortion we absorbed in order to survive. But survival is not the same as living, and healing is not about perfection—it's about returning. Returning to the truth of who we were before the world told us otherwise.

This journey is about sovereignty. It's about reclaiming your authenticity—the highest frequency there is. It's about understanding the quantum nature of belief – that every thought emits a signal, and every signal attracts a match. It's about making peace with your past, without being defined by it. It's about '*re-genre-ing*' our stories and breaking the loops.

Awareness doesn't erase conditioning.

It shortens its lifespan.

Chapter 1

Discovering your unbalanced beliefs

Before we can rewrite/re-genre our stories, we first need to see the beliefs that have been shaping them. The questions below are designed to help you gently uncover some of the core – often unconscious – beliefs that may be driving your thoughts, feelings and patterns. These examples are not exhaustive. For now, allow these prompts to guide your awareness, not from a place of judgment, but from a place of deep curiosity and self-compassion.

As you move through these questions, tune into your gut responses. Don't overthink. Highlight or note the ones that bring up emotion, defensiveness or deep recognition – they're pointing to a core belief you may be holding.

Belief: 'I'm not enough'

- Do you often feel like you're falling short, no matter how hard you try?

- Is there a quiet drive to constantly prove yourself, or improve yourself?
- Do compliments make you uncomfortable, or feel untrue?
- Do you compare yourself to others and come up lacking?
- When something goes wrong, do you assume it's because *you didn't do enough*?

Belief: 'I'm unlovable'

- Do you feel love must be earned, not freely given? Do you fear people will eventually see the 'real' you…and not want you, or leave?
- Have you ever stayed in relationships where you weren't really met or cherished?
- Do you secretly believe you're too much – or not enough – to be loved as you are?
- Does receiving affection or kindness feel suspicious or undeserved?

Belief: 'I'm defective' / 'Something is wrong with me'

- Do you hide parts of yourself for fear they'll be judged or rejected? Do you feel fundamentally flawed, broken or unlike others?
- When someone criticises you, does it feel like confirmation of a deep fear?

Belief: 'I don't matter' / 'I'm invisible'

- Do you struggle to speak up, set boundaries or ask for what you need?
- Have you often felt overlooked, ignored or left out?
- When you're hurting, do you feel like no one notices, or cares?
- Do you suppress your needs, so others won't be burdened?
- Has it felt like your presence or absence doesn't make a difference?

Belief: 'I'm not safe' / 'The world is dangerous'

- Are you hypervigilant or always anticipating worst-case scenarios?
- Do you have difficulty relaxing, even when things are going well?
- Do you avoid vulnerability or closeness because it feels risky?
- Did you learn that trusting others often led to hurt or disappointment?
- Is your nervous system constantly 'on' or wired for survival?

Belief: 'I have to earn my worth' / 'My value is in what I do'

- Do you base your self-worth on productivity, achievements, or being needed?
- Is rest or receiving support difficult or guilt-inducing for you?
- Are you uncomfortable when you're not 'doing' or contributing?
- Have you taken on a caretaker, helper, or overachiever role to feel valued?
- Do you feel only as good as your last success?

Which set of questions brought up the most emotional charge, resistance, or truth?

This is not about blame.

It's about bringing light to what has been living in the shadows.

What this chapter revealed for you – Use this space to record what resonated, what shifted, what landed.

Chapter 2

The Seed of Not Enough

Most people don't walk around saying, *'I feel unworthy'.* But you can see it in their eyes. You feel it in their relationships. You notice it in the subtle ways they abandon themselves to be chosen or shrink to be acceptable.

The belief *'I am not enough'* doesn't live in words. It lives in behaviours, in nervous system responses, in the stories we tell and the ones we avoid.

It can *sound* like an endless inner loop whispering, '*I should've done more'*, or '*they probably don't like me'.* It might say, '*once I lose weight (or get the promotion, or finally heal), then I'll be okay'.* It might convince you that you're too much or not enough. That you shouldn't be a burden, should be more grateful, that others will leave once they really know you, or that everything that goes wrong is somehow your fault. It tells you happiness will come later, after you've fixed yourself.

It can *feel* like living in quiet tension. You over-apologise or over-explain, chasing reassurance that never lands. You hold impossibly high standards, calling them self-discipline, but they're really self-doubt in disguise. You say *yes* when your body screams *no*. You stay in relationships where you're not chosen, overachieve without feeling fulfilled, compare yourself to others and only rest when you've earned it. Even your successes hum with the faint vibration of shame or the thought, *I should be past this by now.*

And yet, most of this is invisible. On the outside, you might look capable, kind, even confident. You've built a life others admire, but inside – there's a constant frequency of striving. A pull to improve, fix, earn, prove.

You're not alone. This is one of the most universal human wounds. It begins early, long before we had words for it.

Where It Begins...

No child is born feeling 'not enough'.

We arrive as pure awareness – curious, connected, present, thinking and feeling we are amazing and lovable – but very early, we start absorbing the emotional climate of our family, school and social world.

You don't need to have experienced trauma in the traditional sense. Sometimes it's the subtle, chronic invalidations that shape us most. The following are just a few examples:

- Being given too much responsibility for your age – caring for others emotionally or physically before your own needs were ever named.
- A parent too preoccupied, distracted or overwhelmed to notice your joy, your tears or your stories.
- Receiving praise only when you performed well – high grades, perfect behaviour, gold stars – and silence when you simply existed.
- Feeling rejection when you cried 'too much', felt 'too deeply', or took up 'too much' space.
- Becoming the caretaker in a home where love had to be earned – through helpfulness, silence or self-sacrifice.
- Being told 'you're fine' when you clearly weren't – and learning to distrust your own emotional signals.
- Having your boundaries ignored, overruled or minimised – teaching you that your *no* didn't matter.
- Being labelled 'difficult', 'dramatic' or 'attention-seeking' when you were simply needing connection.
- Never being asked what *you* needed – only being told what was expected.
- Parents who were loving but emotionally unavailable – physically present but not attuned.
- Subtle glances, sighs or comments that implied you were a disappointment, even when nothing was said outright.
- Learning early that being *good* meant being small – agreeable, quiet, low-maintenance.

- Growing up in a home where no one talked about emotions – where silence replaced support.
- Always being the 'resilient one', which became code for 'no one checks if you're okay'.
- Absorbing the belief that love must be earned, worth must be proven and needs are burdens.

But the classroom, too, can plant this seed.

- Being compared to others – the 'top of the class' vs 'must try harder' dynamic that quietly ranks your worth.
- Punished for daydreaming, asking too many questions or simply not fitting into the system's rigid mould.
- Told 'you're too much', 'too chatty', 'too loud' – or 'not trying hard enough', 'not living up to your potential'.
- Being misunderstood because you were sensitive, deeply feeling, imaginative, neurodivergent or simply wired differently.
- Trying hard to belong – through effort, conformity, silence – and still feeling like you never quite made the mark.
- Internalising the red pen, the grades, the frowns – as reflections of who you are, not just what you did.
- Feeling anxious before presentations, freezing during tests or disassociating when overwhelmed – but no one noticing.

- Learning that your value was tied to performance, obedience or being liked – not presence, curiosity or authenticity.
- Being praised only when you achieved and overlooked when you simply were.
- Feeling the sting of exclusion – not being picked, not being invited, not being seen.
- Becoming the good girl, the class clown, the overachiever, the rebel – not because it was who you truly were, but because it was how you coped.
- Learning early that safety meant pleasing, hiding or proving – never just existing.

School environments often reward performance, compliance and sameness – while silently shaming difference, emotion or unmeasurable gifts. For many, the message becomes clear: *To be worthy, I must be what they want.*

We make meaning quickly as children. We personalise everything. If love, safety or praise was inconsistent, we didn't question the system—we questioned ourselves.

'If I was just better – quieter, smarter, faster, funnier - then maybe I'd feel loved, safe or enough.'

And from there, the pattern sets in.

Why This Wound Persists

As adults, we often recreate the environments we knew – not because they're good, but because they're familiar. We choose relationships where we feel we must earn love. We over function to feel safe. We reject parts of ourselves to avoid rejection from others. We use people and situations to validate our worth. It's not because we're broken; it's because the nervous system believes it's safer to repeat the pattern than to risk vulnerability.

Healing doesn't start with changing the pattern. It starts with seeing the pattern, without judgment.

Sophie

Sophie was 8 when she missed a word in the spelling test. She had studied all week, whispering each word at the kitchen table while her mum hurried between phone calls and dinner. She got 19 out of 20. Almost perfect. Her dad tapped the page and said, 'which one did you miss?'.

It wasn't the first time she felt that drop in her stomach. She remembered the Christmas concert when she scanned the crowd, hoping for her mum's smile, but found her talking to a neighbour and missing Sophie's solo, or the netball game when she blocked the winning shot, but her coach only said she needed to 'run harder next time'. Or the time she brought home a drawing, proud of the swirl of colour, only to hear, 'That's nice, but don't leave your mess on the table'.

None of these moments were dramatic, but together they wrote a story: try harder, be better, don't disappoint.

At school, the pattern deepened. She learned that the children who were quiet, neat and predictable were praised, while the ones who daydreamed, cried easily or asked too many questions were corrected. Sophie worked hard to be the good girl, the reliable one. She smiled even when she was upset. She raised her hand with the right answer. She never wanted to be the one who needed too much.

By the time Sophie was a teenager, the wound had shaped the way she showed up with friends. She laughed along with the jokes even when they hurt. She apologised when she hadn't done anything wrong. She compared herself silently, always measuring and always coming up short.

When she fell in love for the first time, she carried that same ache into romance. She wanted to be chosen so badly that she bent herself small to fit. She said *yes* when she meant *no*. She stayed even when she felt unseen. When her boyfriend pulled away, she didn't ask why. She just worked harder to keep him.

As an adult, the loop was harder to see but just as present. At work, Sophie was praised for being competent, dependable, always available – but she stayed late while others went home, quietly picking up the tasks no one else wanted. When her boss overlooked her for a promotion, she didn't complain. She told herself she should have done more.

In love, the pattern repeated again. She dated men who were half-present, and instead of leaving she over gave, convinced that if she was more patient, more kind, more everything, one day they would finally deeply choose her. Deep down, she knew the distance hurt, but part of her colluded with it. Staying felt safer than leaving. Working harder felt easier than asking for more.

On the outside, Sophie was admired. On the inside, she was exhausted. She didn't have the words for it then. She only knew the sharp edge of striving, the quiet hum of shame beneath every success.

Your Soul Already Knows

You are not your pattern.

You are not your past.

You are not the child who learned to strive for love.

You are the awareness that can witness all of this now.

And here's the good news: Once you see the belief clearly, it no longer runs the show unconsciously. *Awareness is alchemy.*

Sovereignty Takeaway

What you learned was never the truth of you. You are not the wound you absorbed. You are the one who can now choose a new story.

Gentle Reflection

Take a moment. Breathe.

Let this be a quiet conversation with your heart.

Ask yourself:

- When did I first begin to feel like I wasn't enough?
- What did 'being enough' seem to depend on?
- In what ways do I still try to earn love, approval, or safety?
- Were there moments in school where I felt humiliated, left out, or unseen?
- What did I come to believe about myself as a result of those early experiences?

Let whatever rises come gently. There is nothing to fix. Just notice. Witnessing is enough.

What this chapter revealed for you – Use this space to record what resonated, what shifted, what landed.

Patterns don't die quietly.

They check whether they still have access.

Chapter 3

The Pattern Revealed

Until you make the unconscious conscious, it will direct your life, and you will call it fate

— Carl Jung

The belief 'I am not enough' rarely stays hidden. It weaves itself into your thoughts, your relationships, your ambitions and your silences. It can wear a thousand masks: overachievement, self-doubt, people-pleasing, emotional withdrawal, control. But it always stems from the same wound, a part of you that once decided, *'There must be something wrong with me.'*

How the Pattern Plays Out

No two people express this wound in the same way, but the thread is familiar.

In relationships, you might over-give, hoping to be chosen, or stay silent rather than express your needs for fear of being abandoned. You may find yourself drawn to emotionally unavailable people and work tirelessly to earn their love. It can feel unsafe to be fully seen, so you present a polished version of yourself. Even neutrality or space can be read as rejection. And when one relationship ends, you might leap straight into another, unable to sit with the ache of emptiness beneath the pattern.

At work, it can look like quiet self-doubt hidden behind competence. You may feel like a fraud, no matter how skilled you are. You work harder than everyone else, yet it never feels like enough. Your worth becomes tied to productivity, impact or praise. You say *yes* when your body screams *no* because you don't want to disappoint, and when success comes, you downplay it, fearing it might set you apart or invite judgment.

In your self-talk, the wound whispers its familiar refrains: *I should be further along. 'What's wrong with me? I can't get it right. Everyone else seems to have it together, why not me?'* These quiet, looping thoughts become the background noise of your days, shaping the choices you make and the way you meet yourself.

It becomes a cycle that keeps looping until we do the work.

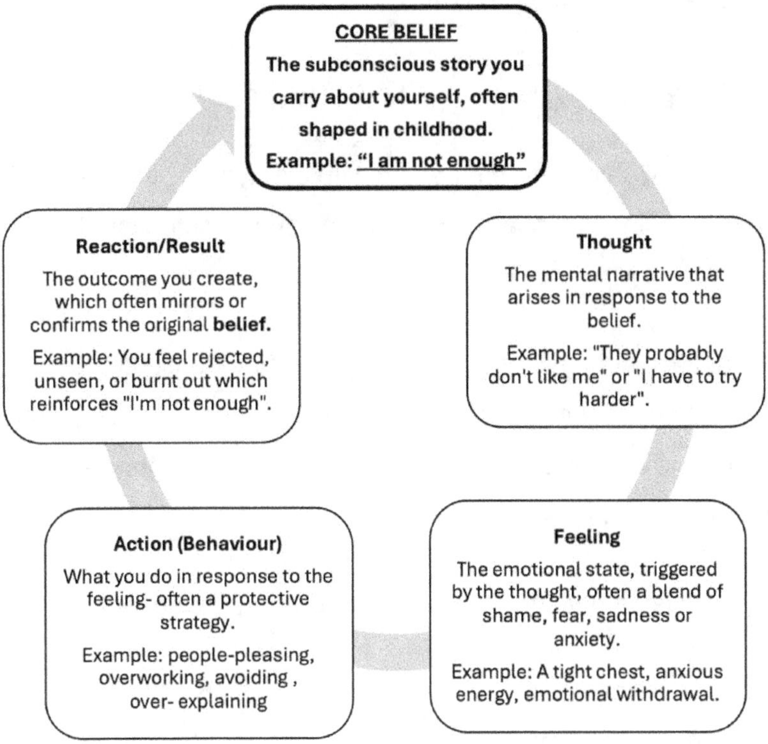

CORE BELIEF

The subconscious story you carry about yourself, often shaped in childhood.

Example: "I am not enough"

Thought

The mental narrative that arises in response to the belief.

Example: "They probably don't like me" or "I have to try harder".

Feeling

The emotional state, triggered by the thought, often a blend of shame, fear, sadness or anxiety.

Example: A tight chest, anxious energy, emotional withdrawal.

Action (Behaviour)

What you do in response to the feeling- often a protective strategy.

Example: people-pleasing, overworking, avoiding , over- explaining

Reaction/Result

The outcome you create, which often mirrors or confirms the original **belief.**

Example: You feel rejected, unseen, or burnt out which reinforces "I'm not enough".

The core beliefs we subconsciously have, give rise to what we think and feel, which drives our actions (behaviour) and our subsequent results, which in turn re-enforces the core belief… and we cycle around.

We begin to live *from* the core belief (wound), not realising we're recreating the very experiences we fear, because we haven't seen the pattern *as a pattern*.

Why Awareness is Everything...

You do not need to fight the pattern. You need to see it.

When you watch your inner world with clarity and compassion, the grip begins to loosen. Awareness disrupts autopilot. It makes choice possible.

In quantum mechanics, the observer effect suggests that observation influences outcomes. When you shift a belief, you change the lens through which you observe, and your life outcomes change accordingly.

But there is something even more fundamental here.

You are not your thoughts.
You are not your emotions.
You are not your body or your history.

You are the one aware of them.

Thoughts arise, emotions move, sensations shift, patterns repeat, but something in you notices all of it. That noticing does not change. That is awareness. That is you.

And this is why awareness is everything. Because the pattern cannot run unconsciously when it is being seen. The moment you become aware, you are no longer fully inside it. You are in relationship with it. And from there, something new becomes possible.

This is not about blaming yourself. It is about empowering yourself.

'I notice I shut down when I feel not enough.'
'I can see I'm trying to earn love by over-functioning or people-pleasing.'
'I'm choosing someone who won't choose me and that's familiar, not fulfilling.'

These are not just insights. They are doorways/portals to liberation.

You are Not Broken - You are Brilliant.

The part of you that developed these patterns was wise. You did what you had to do to feel safe, loved and accepted. You shaped yourself to survive. But survival strategies are not meant to be lifelong identities.

There is nothing wrong with you for having learned them, and there's deep power in learning how to *unlearn* them. The fact that you are here – reading this, asking deeper questions, seeing with new eyes – means something in you is *already* healing.

You are not behind. You are not lost. You are not broken.

You are remembering your wholeness.

Nathan and Elise.

As a young man, Nathan wore charm like armour. He had learned early that to avoid disapproval, it was safer to be agreeable, humorous, the one who always said yes. He became the entertainer, quick with a joke, the man who could make everyone laugh. Women noticed. He could pick them up easily, slipping into light banter, playful confidence, the role of the man who had it together. He had mastered the art of reading the energy and reflecting back what women wanted. A player in the truest sense.

Depth, however, was dangerous. With intimacy came responsibility, and with responsibility came the risk of criticism. Nathan kept things shallow. One-night stands, short flings, affection without commitment. If it started to feel too close, he moved on. Often, he found fault with women almost immediately. Within days, he would convince himself something was wrong with them, and then he would leave. If the mask began to slip, he simply changed the stage.

Then came Elise. She had been doing her own inner work and was drawn to his brightness, the humour, the easy laugh, the endless positivity. Nathan was besotted with her, and to Elise this felt like healing. She had carried the ache of her father's abandonment during her teenage years, and Nathan's devotion struck directly at that wound. To be chosen, to be wanted, to be seen.

In Nathan's attention, Elise felt validated in ways she had longed for. Even when she noticed flashes of incongruence, such as the tension in his body when he pretended everything was fine, or the anger behind his smile, she pushed those observations aside. Being chosen felt too precious to risk. Her pattern was activated as much as his. Where Nathan had learned to avoid, Elise had learned to fix.

When they bought a property together and married the cracks widened. Nathan had agreed with enthusiasm to buy the property, yet when the pressure of responsibility grew, he avoided speaking about it. Instead, he began quietly planning alternatives. Nathan went on a few holidays without Elise, that doubled as reconnaissance missions for him to look at other properties that he might buy and move to without her. While Elise thought they were building a shared life, Nathan was already rehearsing his escape. She eventually found a contract of sale tucked in his bag.

The contract was only one example. Throughout the years, the same loop replayed. Whenever an issue arose, Nathan pushed his feelings down rather than risk Elise's disapproval. He became overwhelmed by the fear that his truth would not be accepted, and his default was to hide it. He withheld, spun stories, told half-truths. Elise, strong and perceptive, always uncovered them. A phone call from a friend, a stray text, a receipt tucked away, another contract in a drawer. Every time the surface story cracked, the deeper truth seeped out.

When she confronted him, Nathan rarely admitted the whole truth at once. He would double down, weave another layer, lie again, until the weight of it became too heavy to hold. Eventually, there would be a confession. He would share how broken he felt, how damaged his childhood had left him, and Elise, who longed to fix and soothe, circled back to comfort him. Rather than asking, 'Why did you lie?', the focus turned into, 'How do I help you feel better?'.

This became their rhythm. Nathan hid and denied. Elise uncovered and forgave. He was caught in avoidance; she was caught in repair. His fear of disapproval and her need to be chosen fused into a cycle that slowly eroded trust and intimacy.

Over time, the relationship became defined not by the love they once felt but by the patterns they could not break. Nathan withdrew into secrecy, mistruths and denial. Elise contorted herself to manage his fragility, soothing his shame while neglecting her own need for honesty, integrity and openness.

Eventually, Elise left the marriage. She recognised both their patterns, his avoidance and her fixing, and saw the loop for what it was: a cycle neither of them could escape. She had used every tool she knew to try to change it, and still the rhythm remained. Leaving was not failure, but awareness. Nathan moved on quickly, finding another partner to fill the space. Elise did not. She chose to remain single for years, not from bitterness, but from intention.

She understood that this relationship had been a mirror, showing her both the ache of her own wound and the limits of her rescuing. She knew that if she simply moved on without pausing, the story would repeat itself again. So, Elise began the work of *re-genreing* her life. No longer a failed romance, but a sovereignty story. A story of returning to herself, remembering her wholeness and choosing connection that aligned with her truth.

In the end, their marriage was not wasted. It was the classroom. Nathan's patterns had shown her her own. Their dynamic had revealed what still needed healing. For Elise, the re-genre was not about erasing the past but about reclaiming it, transforming the old script of avoidance and fixing into a new story of sovereignty and self-honouring.

Maya

On Monday morning, Maya's boss popped his head into her office. 'Could you take this presentation? The deadline's been moved forward.' 'Of course', she said, even though her week was already full. She stayed late, sent it off, and told herself it was no big deal. When the *thank you* email went to the team and not to her, she smiled and said it didn't matter. It did.

By Wednesday, her jaw ached from clenching. A colleague made a joke in a meeting that landed on her like a dig. She laughed along because everyone else did. On the way back to her desk she heard the old thought rise, 'I should be further along by now'. She swallowed it like a pill.

Thursday night was date night with Aaron, a man who texted good morning and then disappeared for hours. He had said, 'I'm not ready for anything serious,' and she had replied, 'Me neither', even though she was. She bought concert tickets. He cancelled on the day. 'Totally fine', she replied, and meant it for about a minute.

On Saturday she drove to her parents' place to help fix a leaky tap. Her dad inspected her car as if checking a report card. 'You still haven't sorted that scratch.' Her mum asked about work, then offered advice she hadn't asked for. Maya smiled, changed the topic, and washed the dishes before being asked. She left with a container of leftovers and a familiar emptiness she could not name.

None of these moments were dramatic. Together, they made a pattern. A tiny cut, then another, then another. She said *yes* when her body said *no*. She worked harder and went quieter. She tried to earn what she really wanted to receive.

When Aaron pulled away, she filled the silence with effort. She sent the funny reels. She cooked the meal she knew he liked. She told herself he was busy, not distant. When that ache in her chest flared, she treated it like a problem to solve rather than a message to hear. She was not only living the pattern. She was maintaining it.

Work mirrored the same loop. When a new project came up, her boss gave it to the louder staff member in the meeting. 'Makes sense', Maya said, even though she had more experience. Later, she stayed back helping him finish it. He sent her a quick thank you message, and she told herself that was enough.

When things finally ended with Aaron on a Sunday afternoon, she cried for 20 minutes and had opened a dating app by Sunday night. She told herself that starting again quickly meant she was brave. It looked like momentum. It was a bypass. The shape changed. The story stayed.

On a quiet Tuesday, the pattern showed itself with surprising clarity. She was drafting a text to a friend, apologising for taking too long to reply. Her shoulders were up by her ears. Her breath was thin. The words on her phone read, 'Sorry, I'm the worst at texting.' Her chest was tight.

She put the phone down and did nothing for one slow breath. She noticed the urge to fix, to please, to reach first. She could feel the old story tugging on her hand. In that moment, she saw it. Trigger, story, reaction, reinforcement. Not fate. A loop.

She did not change her life that afternoon. She changed one message. She deleted 'Sorry', and wrote, 'Got your text. Thinking of you. Want to catch up on Saturday?' Her body softened. It was small. It was everything. For a second, she was not inside the pattern. She was watching it.

Maya still stayed late at work that week. She still felt the ache when her boss praised someone louder. She still missed Aaron, but now there was a thin line of light through the door. She could see the shape of what she kept choosing and now recognised how she had been holding it in place.

And once you see a pattern as a pattern, it cannot pretend to be your personality anymore. It is just a script you learned. Which means it is a script you can rewrite and re-genre.

Neuro-Shift: Embodying a New Frequency

Visualise yourself free of the belief, 'I am not enough.'

- Close your eyes.
- Breathe into your heart.
- Imagine yourself living from a place of worthiness and wholeness — as if nothing about you needs to be fixed, proven, or earned.

Reflect on this version of you:

- How would you stand?
- How would you speak?
- What would you no longer tolerate?
- What kind of relationships would you attract?
- What energy would you broadcast?

Let your body feel that version of you. Embody it now.

Write it into being. Complete this statement:

I am_________________________________enough.

e.g 'I am smart enough, I am attractive enough.'

Who would you be? How would you show up? What choices would you make from this knowing?

Now choose a recent scenario where the belief 'I'm not enough' was triggered.

How did you respond? *(Write freely in the space below)*

If you were anchored in the frequency of 'I am enough'...

- What new thoughts would you have had?
- What behaviours would you choose instead?
- What boundaries would you honour?

(Reflect and write your response below)

This is how you begin to change your state. And when your frequency shifts, your reality begins to reflect it.

Sovereignty Takeaway

Beliefs shape behaviour. Behaviour repeats the wound. Awareness interrupts the loop. Patterns test access.

Gentle Reflection – on your current loops (thoughts, feelings, behaviours)

Ask yourself:

- In what areas of my life do I feel like I'm not enough?
- Where do I notice myself repeating the same painful patterns?
- What behaviours do I return to that leave me feeling drained, resentful, or unseen?
- What do I fear would happen if I stopped trying so hard?
- Can I witness these patterns without judging myself?

If you're ready to go deeper, gently ask:

- What does my body feel or do when I'm caught in this pattern?

Breathe. Let whatever rises come with curiosity.

You are not here to fix yourself. You are here to see clearly, gently, and honestly. Compassion is the medicine.

What this chapter revealed for you – Use this space to record what resonated, what shifted, what landed.

Chapter 4

Reclaiming the Part That Believes It's Not Enough

Be the person you needed when you were younger

— Ayesha Siddiqi

By now, you have seen the pattern. You have traced it to early wounds, moments where the message landed: *Who I am is not okay* or *I need to be more, or different, to be loved.* You have noticed how it still shows up, in work, in love, in the quiet corners of your mind.

Now, we turn toward the part of you that still believes it. Not to fix them. Not to shame them. But to meet them with compassion and bring them back into wholeness.

What is Reclaiming?

Reclaiming is the process of becoming the safe, loving, attuned presence your younger self did not consistently receive. It is not about blaming your parents, caregivers, teachers or early partners. It is about taking sacred responsibility now.

It is the act of saying to that younger part of you:

'I see you.'

'You didn't deserve that.'

'You're not too much.'

'You don't need to earn love anymore.'

'You get to rest. I have you now.'

This is the foundation of self-worth. Not affirmations layered over unhealed pain, but a deep, felt sense of: *I am safe to be me; I am worthy because I exist.*

How the Younger Self Shows Up

Your younger self may speak through emotion, not words. They might show up as:

- A panic when someone pulls away
- A need to overexplain yourself
- A shutdown when criticised
- A fear of being seen or felt
- A drive to do, in order to feel valuable.

Each reaction is a signal, a cue, an invitation to pause and listen. This is not irrational. It is historical.

A Simple Reclaiming Practice

The next time you feel triggered, try this:

1. Pause and breathe. Place your hand on your heart or belly. Remind your body: *I am here.*
2. Ask: How old do I feel right now? Noticing this helps you separate present-you from past-you.
3. Speak gently to that younger part of you: *I know this hurts; you are safe now; you are allowed to feel; you do not have to prove anything to be loved.*
4. Let the emotion move. Cry. Breathe. Journal. Shake. Walk. Give the energy space to move through without shame.
5. Return to now. Come back to your adult self, grounded, compassionate and present. The one who can now guide with awareness.

This is not a one-time fix. It is a devotion. A practice. A sacred re-alignment.

You Are Not the Wound,

You Are the Healer

What happened to you matters, but what you believed about yourself because of it is what truly shaped you.

You are not that belief. You are the awareness that can now hold the belief with love and acceptance.

Each time you offer compassion to that younger part of you, instead of abandoning, rejecting or shaming them, you create new neural pathways. You rewire your nervous system. You shift your frequency, and therefore the people, places and experiences shift. You become the kind of presence your younger self longed for.

You are the love you were waiting for. Let this truth live in you. Not as something to strive for, but as something to remember.

A Gentle Invitation

Take 5–10 minutes to write a letter to your younger self, at the age you most remember feeling 'not enough'. What would you say to them now? What do they need to hear? What do you now know that they did not?

Let the words come from your heart. Let them be imperfect. Let them be real.

Because this is the path: From wound, to wisdom, to wholeness. This is not the moment the loop disappears. It's the moment it starts to lose its grip. When you offer your younger self what they never received, the pattern loses its authority.

Emma

Emma was 6 when she learned to read her father's moods before she read her own. If he came home tired and short, she kept her voice quiet and her body small. If her mother sighed when Emma cried, she swallowed her tears and said she was fine. She wanted to be easy. She wanted to be enough.

At 12, she stopped bringing her art projects to the kitchen table. Her teacher had once called her work 'messy', and when her mum agreed, 'Yes, she's always been the messy one,' Emma felt a flush of shame she could not name. She decided neatness mattered more than joy.

By the time she was a teenager, the patterns were already forming. If a friend did not invite her out, Emma told herself she had been too much the week before. She tried harder to fit in, laughed at jokes that landed like little cuts, apologised when she had not done anything wrong.

As an adult, the same ache rose in new forms. When her partner Mark came home quiet after work, her chest tightened. *What did I do wrong?* she wondered, scanning her words from earlier in the day. At work, if her manager frowned at a report, Emma went over it 10 times, convinced she had made a mistake. She often stayed late to fix things no one else noticed, leaving exhausted but still uneasy.

In each moment, she was not just reacting to now. She was reacting to then. The child who once decided she was too messy, too dramatic, too much or not enough was still present.

Emma did not see it at first. She thought it was just who she was: sensitive, insecure, prone to worry. But it was her younger self tugging at her sleeve, saying, *See me. Hear me. Do not leave me behind again.*

Later, Emma would come to understand that these reactions were not flaws, but signals. They were echoes of the moments where she had learned to trade authenticity for approval, expression for acceptance and need for silence.

And later still, she would begin to discover that the part of her who panicked, overexplained or shrank was not a weakness to erase, but a younger self waiting to be cared for. She would learn that reclaiming meant becoming the steady presence she once longed for. To notice the fear, to sit with it, and to say inwardly, *I see you. You are safe now. You do not have to earn love anymore.*

Emma did not have that language yet, but one day she would, and in that remembering, she would realise she was not the wound at all, but she could heal it

The Work for the Inner Child: Rewriting the Internal Script

You can't change what happened, but you can change how you relate to it. This is where the re-genre of your story begins.

Emotional triggers often arise in response to something someone says or does. It might be a tone of voice, a silence, a withdrawal or a perceived rejection, but the real pain doesn't come from the event itself. It comes from how we interpret it through the lens of our past.

These are the moments when old narratives/stories get reactivated and loops reignite.

When that happens, pause.... breathe and gently ask yourself -

What belief is the child part of me holding right now? What belief is the younger, protective part of me holding right now — the part shaped by early experiences of love, safety, and worth? (For example: 'They don't love me', 'I'm being rejected again', 'I'm not enough' or 'I'm too much'.)

These thoughts may not be logical or even the truth, but they are deeply familiar. They were formed long before you had the words to challenge them. Unless you bring them into conscious awareness, they will continue to influence your thoughts, emotions and behaviours.

If you wrote a letter to your younger self earlier, now is a beautiful moment to return to it. You may want to ask a few gentle questions that can help your inner child feel more deeply seen:

- What were you told about yourself that wasn't true? (Early messages from caregivers, teachers, or environments often become internalised beliefs, even when they do not reflect your true nature.)

- What do you want your younger self to know about who they really are? (Offering a truer, kinder perspective helps loosen the grip of those early beliefs and introduces a new internal reference point.)
- What do you forgive them for?
- What new truth do you want to offer them now?

Let your answers come through softly. There is no pressure to get it right. This is not about rewriting the past. It is about meeting it with new eyes and a new frequency.

Carl Jung said, 'Until you make the unconscious conscious, it will direct your life, and you will call it fate.'

This is what healing really means. It is not about forcing yourself to change your reactions. It is about recognising the story, the belief or the pattern that sits beneath them.

Once you see that clearly, things begin to shift. Your thoughts change. Your feelings change, and your reactions begin to change too, not through effort but through understanding.

You don't need to push yourself harder. What you need is space to pause and witness. That witnessing is the beginning of presence. And presence is what allows the story to change. This is where the re-genre begins and the loops start breaking.

Sovereignty Takeaway

The child within you is not broken. They are waiting to be seen, guided and held. The story was survival. The re-genre is sovereignty.

What this chapter revealed for you – Use this space to record what resonated, what shifted, what landed.

Chapter 5

The Frequency of Worthiness

Your story sets your signal, and your signal shapes your reality.

— Marnie Sole.

We live in a vibrational universe. This is not poetry, it is physics. Everything has a frequency: your thoughts, your emotions, your beliefs, and the energy you radiate. Whether you realise it or not, the quality of your life reflects the frequency you are operating from.

Worthiness is not something you achieve. It is a frequency you remember and embody. When someone carries the unconscious belief 'I am not enough', it colours everything. It shapes the story they tell themselves, and that story creates a signal. That signal is the frequency being broadcast, and life mirrors it back through experiences in relationships, finances, health and choices. No matter how much they accomplish, the inner state feels incomplete. When that belief begins to soften, even slightly, the external world reflects the change.

The Mirror Effect

The universe is not punishing or rewarding you. It is mirroring you. It does not decide whether you deserve good or bad. It simply reflects the signal you are sending through your focus and emotional charge.

Think of it like an algorithm. Watch one video online and suddenly your feed fills with more of the same. Not because the algorithm likes or dislikes you, but because you signalled interest. Energy works the same way. When you replay painful experiences, talk about them often or keep them alive in your **attention**, you keep that frequency active. The mirror can only reflect it back.

This is why patterns repeat. This is the mechanism behind our loops. Not because you deserve pain, but because the story and belief running underneath are still broadcasting.

Your Inner Signal

You are like a radio tower. What you consistently think and feel (give attention to) is what you broadcast, and what you broadcast is what you attract. Worthiness has a signal. So does unworthiness.

Daniel

Daniel's life reflected this principle clearly.

He grew up in a home where love felt conditional. His father praised him only when he achieved. His mother was affectionate but distracted, nodding at his stories while folding washing. He absorbed the message: love had to be earned, attention was scarce and achievement was safer than authenticity.

As an adult, Daniel carried this frequency of unworthiness into his relationships. On the surface, he was steady, kind and dependable. Friends admired him. Yet inside, the story still played: *I am not enough to be fully chosen.* That story broadcast a signal into the field, and life mirrored it back.

His first serious partner adored him at the beginning but slowly sought attention elsewhere. Another leaned on him for comfort yet looked beyond him for excitement. Each time, Daniel replayed the events in his mind, analysing what he did wrong, telling himself he had failed. Each replay was not just memory, it was fuel. It strengthened the very frequency of lack he longed to escape. Without realising it, Daniel kept energising the very pattern he wanted to escape. This is how loops circulate.

From the perspective of physics, this makes sense. The quantum field responds to the signal being sent. Daniel's focus and emotional charge created coherence with the wound, not the healing. The observer effect in physics shows that what you bring your attention to changes how reality arranges itself. By focusing on abandonment and betrayal, even in fear of avoiding it, Daniel unintentionally invited the same outcome. This is how loops are reinforced.

Entanglement offers another metaphor. Particles that were once connected remain linked, shifting together even across distance. In the same way, when Daniel carried the frequency of unworthiness, the field around him organised to reflect it. Until he changed the state of his inner world, the outer world could only echo it back.

Daniel's story is not about blame. It is about frequency. His wound was not proof of being broken. It was proof of how powerful the field is in mirroring what we broadcast. Once he began to soften the belief, to embody even a small sense of worthiness, the feedback loop began to change.

The Science of Frequency

Dr. David Hawkins' Map of Consciousness demonstrates that every emotional state carries a measurable vibrational frequency. Shame, guilt and fear resonate at the lower end of the scale, while love, joy and peace resonate at the highest. Worthiness lives in these elevated states, not because you earn them, but because your essence already carries that frequency beneath the conditioning.

Dr. Joe Dispenza's research affirms the same. When you embody the elevated emotions of your desired future before it happens, you begin to rewire your brain and body to match that future. You stop waiting for life to change so that you can feel better. You feel better first, and life begins to change in response.

This is not just psychology. It is quantum mechanics. The moment you generate a frequency internally, it enters the quantum field as energy. The field does not respond to what you hope for; it responds to the signal you emit. The observer effect shows that what is observed changes, depending on how it is observed. Your inner state is the observer. The signal you embody influences what takes shape in your external world.

Entanglement also illustrates this. Particles that were once connected remain linked no matter the distance. Change the state of one, and the other shifts instantly. In the same way, when you change the state of your inner world, the field around you reorganises to reflect it.

Embodying Worthiness

So, the question becomes: *What does worthiness feel like in your body?* Can you practise that feeling now?

It might feel like:

- Calm in your belly
- A softening in your chest
- A quiet confidence
- A sense of *enoughness* in this very moment

You do not have to earn this frequency. You return to it. You are it.

Sovereignty Takeaway

What you believe, you feel. What you feel, you broadcast. What you broadcast, you live. This is how energy keeps returning to the same signal – and loops.

What this chapter revealed for you – Use this space to record what resonated, what shifted, what landed.

Chapter 6

Letting Go of the Old Identity

And the day came when the risk to remain tight in a bud was more painful than the risk it took to blossom

— Anaïs Nin

Every core wound gives rise to a protective identity. The achiever. The perfectionist. The helper. The one who never needs anything. The one who always has it together. The one who's always there for others or relentlessly positive.

These identities formed for a reason: they helped us survive, but eventually, they become a cage.

You might have noticed:

- Burnout from over giving
- Resentment in relationships
- Fear of being fully seen
- Constant doing without deep fulfilment.

The old self is exhausted. It wants to rest.

Sam

Sam grew up in a house where performance was survival. His father, a war veteran, died when Sam was still young. His mother had once been a gifted classical musician with the promise of a remarkable career, but she abandoned that dream for marriage. The loss never left her. It lingered like a shadow and shaped the way she raised her children. Her own unrealised potential became the measure by which she drove them.

Comparison was constant. If she bumped into another parent in the street, Sam would hear about it that night. Their boy runs faster than you. Their daughter scored higher than you. Why can't you keep up?

Marks, grades, trophies — everything was proof of worth. When Sam fell short, she made sure he felt it. Sometimes with cutting words, sometimes with blows.

Sam was the second-born. His sister Claire was socially withdrawn and later diagnosed on the autism spectrum. Claire was considered an embarrassment, so all hopes were placed on him. He was pushed into competitive sport, not because he loved it, but because it was another stage for performance. Every race, every result, was less about the activity itself and more about whether he was enough.

Being dux at school each year was expected. He grew up anxious, scanning for disapproval, bracing for the next comparison and striving for perfection.

When his mother remarried, life did not soften. His new stepfather was wealthy, polished and proud, and his children were always better. At family dinners, Sam's chest tightened before he even walked through the door. He worried about what he wore, what he said, how he held himself. Approval was the currency, and he never had enough of it.

By adulthood, Sam had perfected the mask. He was delightful, charming and endlessly agreeable. Friends admired his positivity. Strangers warmed to him. In social settings, he was the one who lit up the room. But behind the shine was a different story.

To avoid rejection or disapproval, Sam told people what they wanted to hear. He said yes easily, smoothed things over, promised much and then quietly did what he wanted anyway.

The identity that once protected him — the agreeable, ever-positive mask — had become a prison. It earned him admiration, but it cost him authenticity. It kept the peace in the moment, but it eroded his trust in himself.

Change did not arrive as a dramatic revelation. It began in small moments.

His partner at the time, Sarah, noticed the anxiety he carried before family gatherings and gently encouraged him to choose for himself. When he froze in front of the wardrobe, worrying about what would win approval, she would ask, “What do you actually want to wear?”

Together they chose clothes that felt like him, not his mother’s or stepfather’s expectations.

The first time he walked into a family dinner wearing something he had chosen for himself, he braced for the sigh, the raised eyebrow, the inevitable comment.

“Looking very casual today,” his mother remarked.

His chest tightened. But nothing else happened. The world did not collapse. That was the first crack in the armour.

After that, Sarah stood beside him at each family gathering, steadying him as he tested the edges of his old identity. Each time he wore what he wanted, each time he sat through the comments, the disapproval and the familiar sting, he discovered he could survive it.

The anxiety still rose, but it no longer dictated his choices.

Slowly, Sam began to realise that letting go was not about losing himself. It was about loosening the grip of an identity that had ruled him for decades. What had once been survival was slowly becoming choice.

The story he had been living — one written by comparison, approval and performance — was beginning to change. Beneath the mask, there was more to him than achievement. More than pleasing others. And little by little, he was learning he could rewrite it.

Letting the Mask Drop

To let go of these identities is not to become less - it's to become real. Authenticity replaces performance. Presence replaces proving. The old identity is one potential you kept collapsing. When you step out of performance, other potentials become available.

Ask yourself:

What parts of me have been performing? What am I afraid will happen if I stop?

Let the answers come without judgement. This is how the mask begins to melt.

Sovereignty Takeaway

The mask kept you safe. Now safety is presence, not performance. You are free to live as your true self. This is where the pattern dissolves and the loop ends.

Gentle Reflection: Meeting the True Self

1. Write a list of the identities you have worn to stay safe or loved. Examples: The Strong One, The Peacemaker, The Overachiever, The Helper.

2. Beside each one, write:

- What this role protected you from.
- What it cost you.

3. Thank each identity for its service, then let it go, without judgement or resistance.

* Ask: Who am I when I'm not trying to be any of these?

This last question does not require an answer. It creates space. And in that space, the true self returns.

Bonus reflection: Is there any part of me that still feels loyal to this identity? Am I afraid of who I'll be without it?

What this chapter revealed for you – Use this space to record what resonated, what shifted, what landed.

Chapter 7

Creating From the Future, Not the Past

The future is not something we enter.
The future is something we create.

— Leonard Sweet

Most people create their life based on memory. The past defines the present. Old wounds set the emotional tone. Yesterday's beliefs become tomorrow's limits.

What if we flipped it? What if you began living from the version of you who is already healed, whole and aligned?

This is what it means to create from the quantum field. This is how the future becomes *now*.

The Quantum Shift

Dr. Joe Dispenza's pioneering work teaches that when you align thought (intention) with emotion (elevated feeling), you create a new electromagnetic signature. This is how you communicate with the quantum field—the infinite field of potential.

You are not waiting for your future—you're *becoming* it.

Each day becomes a rehearsal of the new self and each moment a choice to return to the old story or embody the new.

Living from Memory vs. Living from Possibility

Most people don't realise they are time-travelling in reverse. They wake up and consult yesterday for instructions on how to feel, who to be, and what to expect. The nervous system scans for familiar threats. The mind reaches for old conclusions. The body prepares for what it has already survived.

This is how the past keeps recreating itself. Not through fate, but through identity.

When your sense of self is organised around who you *were*, your choices, reactions, and tolerances unconsciously vote for the same timeline again and again. This is the loop.

Creating from the future requires a different organising principle. Instead of asking, "What happened before and how do I protect myself now?" you begin to ask, "Who am I becoming, and how would they meet this moment?"

This is not bypassing pain or pretending wounds never existed. It is refusing to let them remain the author of your next chapter.

The future self is not a fantasy. It is a frequency already available in the field of possibility. When you begin to think, feel, and act from that identity, the body receives new instructions, the nervous system recalibrates, and behaviour naturally reorganises.

This is how re-genreing becomes lived, not just imagined. You stop casting yourself in a survival story and start moving as the one who has already healed. Not because life is suddenly perfect, but because your centre of gravity has shifted. You are no longer reacting from who you were. You are responding as who you are becoming. And this is how timelines change.

Sovereignty Takeaway

The past is memory, which no longer exists, not destiny. Your future self already exists in the field. The re-genre is choosing to live as them now.

Memory = identity loop

Future self = new organising frequency

Choice = timeline selection

Gentle Reflection: Future Self Activation

1. Sit in stillness. Breathe deeply into your heart and belly.

2. Bring to mind the version of yourself who:

- Feels deeply worthy
- Is in aligned relationships
- Speaks clearly, lives freely, and chooses wisely
- Shows up as their most authentic self

3. Step into that identity. Ask:

- How does this version walk?
- What do they no longer tolerate?
- What do they know that you are still learning?

4. Let your body feel the future. Allow the energy of this version of you to move through your posture, breath, and presence. Ask yourself:

- What new behaviours does this version of me engage in?
- What one action can I take today to honour this self?

This is not imagination. This is the new self being installed, now.

This is not fantasy. This is identity re-patterning in real time. This is the moment the future stops being a concept and becomes a way of moving through the world.

What this chapter revealed for you – Use this space to record what resonated, what shifted, what landed.

Chapter 8

Aligned Relationships – Love Without Losing Yourself

A healthy relationship is one where two people can grow individually and together at the same time

— Unknown

The old wound often leads to relationships based on need and dependency, not alignment. When our worthiness feels fragile, we don't always choose people from wholeness. We choose from ache. From fear. From a subconscious pull to re-enact what hurt us—hoping this time it might end differently.

We become magnetised to people who mirror our original pain:

- The emotionally unavailable partner or friend, echoing the parent who couldn't attune to us.
- The one we have to work hard to keep, reinforcing the belief that love and loyalty must be earned.
- The one who needs fixing or saving, which feeds the identity of being valuable only when we're useful.

- The one who criticises, dismisses or excludes us – validating the story that we're not enough as we are.

These dynamics don't just play out in romance – they show up everywhere: In the friend who takes and never gives. In the boss who manipulates with charm or control. In the group where you feel like you always have to prove your worth or keep your brilliance dialled down. In the colleague you over-function for, hoping they'll finally see you. In the family member whose approval still tugs at your nervous system, no matter how old you are.

We adapt ourselves in subtle ways:

- Becoming the 'funny one' to avoid vulnerability.
- Playing the helper so we don't have to ask for help.
- Staying silent to keep the peace.
- Being the one everyone leans on, while no one really sees you.

But when we begin to embody our worth, something shifts. We start making choices from alignment, not from attachment. We begin to ask: *Does this connection honour who I am becoming? Or who I had to be to feel safe?*

We no longer settle. We seek resonance, not rescue. We become less interested in being chosen – and more devoted to choosing ourselves. Aligned relationships do not complete you – they expand you. They honour your autonomy, your truth, and your becoming.

What Alignment Feels Like (In Any Relationship)

Alignment isn't about finding 'perfect' people. It's about co-creating dynamics where truth, growth and integrity are present.

In aligned friendships, work partnerships or family dynamics, it feels like:

- **You don't have to earn your place.** You are accepted as you are – not for how much you do, or how small you can make yourself.
- **Mutual respect, not power play.** Your voice matters. You're not dismissed, managed or manipulated.
- **Reciprocity.** You're not the only one holding space, initiating, giving. The energy flows both ways
- **Authenticity over performance.** You don't need a mask to be included. You can bring your full self – even when you're in process.
- **Growth is welcomed.** They don't expect the past version of you. They meet the present one – and celebrate the changes.

- **Space to evolve.** You're not frozen in an old role or identity. You're seen as dynamic, evolving and worthy of support along the way.
- **Boundaries are respected.** You don't have to explain or justify your limits. You're met with understanding – not guilt or pushback.
- **There's room for realness.** Laughter, truth, discomfort and even disagreement – all can exist without rupture.
- **You feel safe in your nervous system.** Your body doesn't brace around them. It relaxes.

Aligned relationships do not complete you, they expand you. They honour your autonomy and your evolution.

And in Romantic Partnership?

All of the above still applies – but in deeper, more intimate ways.

Aligned partnership feels like:

- **Freedom to be fully yourself.** No shrinking, performing or proving.

- **Shared growth and evolution.** You walk your own paths, but in chosen partnership.
- **Emotional safety and open communication.** There's space for truth – even when it's uncomfortable.
- **Passion and presence.** There's aliveness without chaos. Intimacy without volatility.
- **Mutual respect and reciprocity.** No emotional labour imbalance. No silent contracts. No unspoken resentment.
- **You don't lose yourself – you return to yourself.** This love doesn't ask you to abandon you. It reflects you back to yourself, whole.

Whether it's a friend, lover, boss, sibling or soul connection… alignment is a frequency, not a role. It's the energy of truth, safety and shared expansion. When you stop abandoning yourself, your relationships recalibrate. Some fall away. Some deepen. But what remains is real. And what is real, expands.

Rowan

Rowan is a man organised around avoidance, not intimacy. He is not reckless with relationships. He is strategic. He does not leave long gaps between connections, but he also does not rush into commitment. Instead, he moves laterally. One woman fades, another appears. Sometimes overlapping. Sometimes staggered. The details change, but the function remains the same. He is rarely without access to female attention, affection, or validation.

From the outside, it can look like healing. Like momentum. Like someone who knows himself. Rowan can speak about his wounds. He understands attachment language. He can name his patterns with just enough insight to sound conscious.

What he has not done is interrupt them.

Being alone long enough to actually meet himself is the one thing he consistently avoids. Because in silence, the old beliefs surface. I am not enough. I do not really matter. I will be exposed if I am truly known. For Rowan, solitude is not restorative. It is dysregulating. So, connection becomes regulation.

This is where the pattern sharpens.

Rowan does not simply move from woman to woman. He accumulates them. Over time, he builds a network of women he has slept with, emotionally bonded with, or partially chosen. When intimacy peaks and discomfort follows, he does not end the connection cleanly. He repositions it.

Women are moved from centre stage to the wings. From intimacy to access.

They are kept tethered through intermittent contact. A warm reply. A flirt. A familiar joke. A check-in that arrives just as they are about to detach. Not enough to move forward. Not enough to let go. Just enough to maintain availability.

What begins as a harem becomes a fan club.

These women function as emotional reserves. Stored sources of affirmation, desire, and reassurance. When Rowan feels ungrounded, unseen, or rejected, he pulls on the tether. Someone returns. Sometimes several. Not because the connection has transformed, but because his need has resurfaced.

This is not intimacy. It is emotional regulation through access.

He is not choosing between women. He is choosing relief over responsibility.

Rowan often believes he is being honest. He says things like, “I’m not ready,” or “I don’t want to hurt anyone.” But these statements function less as accountability and more as disclaimers. They absolve him internally while transferring the emotional labour outward. Awareness, in this form, becomes a loophole.

He is not malicious. He does not set out to harm. But impact does not require intent. And self-knowledge without behavioural change still causes damage.

Eventually, the loop tightens. It always does. Because without addressing the core wound, *I am not enough*, Rowan's nervous system will default back to what is familiar, not what is healthy. When intimacy deepens, he distances. When repair is required, he distracts. When discomfort rises, he reaches outward instead of inward. Not because he does not want connection. But because connection, without escape routes, still feels unsafe.

And then there is the woman he is with now.

Laura is kind. She is emotionally articulate. She is known and well regarded. People describe her as warm, capable, easy to be with, 'lovely'. Being with her reflects well on Rowan. It gives him status. It places him beside someone admired, stable, socially approved and for a man who cares deeply about how he is perceived, this matters.

Laura is sincere. She wants connection. She names her needs clearly. She asks for presence, consistency, and emotional availability. She does not hide what she hopes for.

Rowan tells her, calmly and repeatedly, that he cannot give those things.

Each time this happens, there is a small rupture. A pause. A distancing. Sometimes days. Sometimes weeks. In those spaces, Laura tries to hold her ground. She tells herself she deserves more. She attempts to stay aligned with what she wants.

And then she folds.

Not dramatically. Not consciously. Gently. Reasonably. She softens. She reframes. She lowers the bar and tells herself it is maturity, flexibility, understanding, spiritual. She agrees to less closeness, less clarity, less commitment in order to keep the connection. She's even prepared to accept him sleeping with other women, as long as she doesn't know about it.

This becomes the pattern.

She asks. He declines. There is space. Then she adapts.

What looks like compromise is actually self-abandonment.

Laura believes she is being loving. What she is really doing is regulating him. Her willingness to accommodate removes the very tension that would force Rowan to confront his avoidance. Her patience soothes his nervous system. Her flexibility protects him from the discomfort of change.

She becomes the emotional buffer between his unhealed wounds and the consequences of them.

Laura is not chosen because she challenges him. She is chosen because she makes things easy and provides status.

She does not demand sustained accountability. She does not insist on repair when he withdraws. She accepts partial presence and intermittent closeness and tells herself it is enough for now. In doing so, she becomes the safe harbour that allows the loop to continue uninterrupted.

This is the performer role.

The woman who keeps the peace. The woman who stays pleasant and likeable. The woman who absorbs disappointment quietly and calls it understanding.

Rowan's nervous system settles with Laura because nothing in her requires him to grow. She offers companionship without confrontation, affection without expectation, closeness without consequence. She is the perfect refuge for a man who wants intimacy without transformation.

Laura is not the problem. She is the permission.

How this pattern was shaped

Rowan did not invent avoidance in adulthood. He adapted to it early.

He grew up in a family where provision and presence existed, but emotional attunement did not. Conflict was common. Emotions were managed, not met. Vulnerability was tolerated only briefly before being minimised or redirected.

The message was subtle but consistent. Feel it privately. Handle it yourself. Do not need too much.

This kind of childhood emotional neglect is easy to miss because it hides inside good enough families. Needs are met. Parents show up. But when emotions are repeatedly dismissed, the child learns to suppress rather than process.

Rowan internalised this as a relational blueprint.

Stay independent. Do not rely too deeply. Keep your inner world protected. And beneath it all, closeness requires self-abandonment.

As an adult, intimacy activates this conditioning. He longs for closeness but becomes overwhelmed by emotional demand. Other people's feelings feel intrusive. Repair feels exposing. So, he manages intimacy the way he learned to manage emotions, by containing, compartmentalising, and controlling access.

Rowan does not lack the capacity for love. He lacks safety in sustained emotional presence.

Until that changes, his relationships will continue to orbit the same loop. Not because he is unwilling to grow, but because growth requires a level of aloneness and accountability he has not yet chosen.

Sovereignty Takeaway

You are not here to be completed; you are here to be expanded. When you honour yourself, love becomes a reflection of truth. The story was sacrifice; the re-genre is sovereignty.

Gentle Reflection: Relationship Check-In

- Are you this person, or have you been this person in the past?
- Are you involved with someone like Rowan or have you been?

Take a quiet moment. Breathe deeply. Let this be an honest, loving check-in with your heart.

- Do you feel more like yourself in this relationship, or less?

- Can you be honest, vulnerable and imperfect, and still feel seen?
- Do you believe your emotions truly matter in this connection, or do you silence them to keep the peace?
- Are you choosing from a place of wholeness, or from an unhealed wound?
- Did this connection begin from a space of alignment, or from a desire to soothe, fix or escape?
- Did you move into this relationship as a reaction to the last one?
- Have you gone to the opposite extreme, hoping to find balance, but skipped the healing in between?
- Are you trying to earn love, or are you simply allowing yourself to receive it?
- Do you feel like you need to perform, please or prove something in order to be wanted?
- Does this relationship affirm your *enoughness*, or does it mirror the old belief that you are not enough?
- Are you growing together, or holding each other back?
- Is there mutual support for evolution, or do you find yourself shrinking to keep the peace?

Now turn inward and reconnect with what love truly feels like for you.

Write a vision for your ideal relationship. Let it be based not on a checklist of traits, but on a feeling.

Ask yourself:

- How do I want to feel in love, in intimacy and in connection?
- What kind of energy do I want to live in and co-create with another?

Use the space below and the next page...

Let this vision become your compass. Not something to chase or perfect, but something to return to whenever you lose your way.

You are allowed to want depth, reciprocity, safety and joy. You are allowed to wait for it. You are allowed to walk away from anything that feels like less.

What this chapter revealed for you – Use this space to record what resonated, what shifted, what landed.

Chapter 9

Living As the Healed Self

Your task is not to seek for love, but merely to seek and find all the barriers within yourself that you have built against it

— Rumi

Healing is not a destination – it's a way of being. Living as the healed self means you respond, relate and create from wholeness, not wounding. As you become the awareness – and the newer version of yourself – further layers of awareness may arise.

You will still get triggered. You will still forget, but you return faster. You stay kinder. You catch the old patterns before they run the show. You stop making meaning from your pain. You stop chasing closure in places that can't give it. You no longer need people to behave differently for you to feel free. You don't get pulled into every storm because you know what peace feels like now. You don't bypass emotion – but you no longer drown in it either. You welcome discomfort as an invitation, not a threat. You grieve with grace. You rest without guilt. You honour your intuition, even when it's inconvenient. You no longer see triggers as failures – but as doorways. Doorways to meet another part of yourself with love. You stop asking, *'What's wrong with me?'.* And start asking, *'What does this part of me need to feel safe, seen, and whole?'.* You become the one you needed. Not just in theory, but in practice.

As you become the awareness – not just the reaction, the identity or the narrative – further layers of truth arise.

You realise healing is less about fixing and more about *unfolding*. It's not about becoming someone new. It's about remembering who you were before the world convinced you to forget.

Anchoring Wholeness

This is where practice becomes embodiment. You no longer just *know* you are enough; you live it.

You walk into rooms differently.

You speak to yourself with reverence.

You make decisions that honour your nervous system and soul.

You no longer abandon yourself for approval.

You stop seeking love through sacrifice.

You choose connection that uplifts, not contracts.

Anchoring wholeness looks like:

- Saying no without explanation.
- Saying yes without guilt.
- Trusting your body when it signals 'not this'.
- Creating space before reacting.
- Noticing the pause – and choosing the response.
- Letting your joy be loud.
- Letting your rest be sacred.

You move from hypervigilance to presence. From proving to receiving. From protection to openness.

Wholeness isn't about always feeling good – it's about being rooted even when things feel hard. It's about trusting that your worth isn't fragile. That your truth doesn't need defending. That your belonging doesn't require betrayal.

You are no longer the fractured self, trying to be enough. You are the sovereign self, living like it already is.

Grace

Grace grew up in a home where love was uneven, always tilted one way or another. One parent over-loved her, smothering her with intensity, while the other was physically present yet emotionally unavailable. She went from being left alone to being engulfed. The contrast carved a deep confusion in her small body: *Am I too much, or am I not enough?*

That question became the frequency beneath her choices.

As a woman, the pattern threaded itself through her relationships. She was drawn to men who were magnetic but unavailable, men who pulled her close with intensity, even obsession, and then slipped away, not physically, but emotionally. They struggled to be vulnerable, to stay present in the depth of intimacy. She was fulfilling all of their needs so they stayed in the relationship, and she would always stay in the relationship even though she was not happy.

Each time she told herself that if she loved enough, stayed patient enough, softened enough, she could fix it. She believed that if she could hold the relationship steady, it would finally fill the gap carved in her early years.

Her presence was striking. Tall, magnetic, self-contained, she carried the energy of someone who seemed untouchable. People admired her strength, yet few saw the tender spaces she guarded within. Men were intrigued, often magnetised, but eventually they echoed the same dynamic she had known since childhood: there but not there.

Years of inner work began to shift the trajectory. Grace traced her choices back to the child who had grown up oscillating between suffocation and neglect – rescuing and soothing. She saw how she had replayed that same contradiction through the men she chose. Slowly, she began to catch herself in the spiral. She did not bypass the ache or deny it, yet she learned to circle back to her centre with more speed and more grace each time.

Living as her healed self, did not mean she never got triggered. When a man she cared for pulled away emotionally, her chest still tightened. The old urge to prove herself, to bend smaller, to work harder still rose. Now she recognised the echo for what it was: history replaying itself. She could pause, place a hand on her heart, and remind herself – *I am already enough. I do not need to earn love.*

Her healing looked like a spiral. She rose into sovereignty, dipped back into old wounds, and circled upward again. Each time she returned, she landed higher. Not perfect, but steadier.

Grace no longer drowned when the old stories surged. She could float, breathe and let the wave pass. She no longer needed feedback or validation at work or in relationships to prove her worthiness. Her sense of *enoughness* came from remembering who she was before the early program was installed. Full circle, back to the child who had arrived whole.

Perfection had lost its hold. Grace no longer demanded it from herself, and she no longer sought it in others. Living as the healed self was not about waiting for a perfect partner; it was about no longer choosing those who required rescuing. She could welcome someone flawed, human, still learning, as long as he met her with truth and authenticity.

In friendships, she stopped apologising for her boundaries. At work, she spoke from authenticity and sovereignty, rather than striving for approval. In love, she began to choose differently, not abandoning herself for intensity, not confusing attention with presence.

Living as her healed self did not erase her wounds. It gave her a new relationship with them. The old stories still knocked, yet they no longer owned the house. Grace had become the awareness – the one who could meet each trigger with compassion and return to truth.

She discovered wholeness was not fragile. It was steady. It was hers.

<u>Sovereignty Takeaway</u>

Living healed is not perfection, it is presence. You return to yourself again and again, softer each time. The story was striving, the re-genre is remembering.

Gentle Reflection: Daily Integration

Morning Prompt:

Ask, *'How would my healed self show up today?'*

- Today, I will honour myself by…
- If I notice myself slipping into autopilot, I will pause and…

Evening Reflection:

Reflect, *'Where did I honour myself today? Where did I abandon myself?'*

Then bring compassion to both.

- I honoured myself today by…
- I abandoned myself when…
- What does this part of me need to feel safe and seen?
- Tomorrow, I will honour myself by

This is the rhythm of re-alignment.

Not perfection – presence.

Mantra

I am already whole. I walk in truth, I rest in safety, I love from fullness. This is who I am, not because I earned it, but because I remembered.

What this chapter revealed for you – Use this space to record what resonated, what shifted, what landed.

Chapter 10

The Wisdom in Your Wound

Every person, experience, and emotion arrives as a teacher, inviting your evolution.

— Marnie Sole

If you have ever asked, 'Why is this happening to me?' you're not alone. But perhaps a more powerful question is:

'What is this experience here to show me?'

There is a deeper intelligence at work in every challenge we face – an inner curriculum designed not to punish us, but to *evolve* us. Our most painful moments are not detours from our purpose—they are the very *path* to it.

From Pain to Purpose

Pain wakes us up. It calls our attention to what has been suppressed, avoided, or unconsciously repeated. And though it often arrives wrapped in discomfort, pain always brings a message. A message from the soul.

Take the core wound **'I am not enough'.** It might originate from early experiences - feeling unseen in a busy household, receiving love only when achieving, or being criticised for simply being oneself. These moments plant a seed of self-doubt, which can quietly grow into adulthood, influencing every relationship, goal and self-perception.

This belief might drive someone to over-perform, to be the fixer in relationships, or to silence their own needs to stay safe and liked. They might achieve success externally yet still feel empty internally.

Eventually, life will mirror this inner wound loud enough that it cannot be ignored – through burnout, betrayal, failed relationships or a deep, aching loneliness. It is in that breaking point that something shifts.

You begin to question the belief.

What if I was never supposed to earn my worth? What if I am – and always was – enough?

That crack in the narrative lets the light in. You begin to set boundaries. To rest. To express. To stop abandoning yourselves for others. And through that healing process, wisdom is born.

Breaking the Loop

Healing does not erase our wounds – it transforms how we carry them. That same person who once felt unworthy may now become a compassionate mentor, an advocate for authenticity or a gentle space-holder for others feeling lost.

Their purpose isn't found in perfection, but in presence. Their pain has become their compass.

We often think purpose is something we *find* – but more often, it's something we *remember*. It's revealed as we unravel everything that told us we were not enough. Our purpose is born from the wisdom of our unique journey.

The Gift Inside the Struggle

Everything we experience – yes, even the grief, confusion, betrayal and failure – is part of our soul's evolution. Life isn't random. It's a mirror, constantly reflecting the places within us that long to be seen, loved and liberated.

Growth doesn't come from comfort. It comes from being stretched beyond what we thought we could handle and discovering we are more powerful, compassionate and conscious than we ever knew.

Your wounds are not your shame—they are your training grounds.

Your pain is not the opposite of your purpose—it is the path to it.

A Personal Reflection from Marnie –

The Pattern Beneath the Pain

When I was around 14, my mother was in and out of psychiatric care. She was unwell – plagued by anxiety, panic attacks and waves of depression I couldn't understand at the time. One moment she was home, and the next she was gone. No explanations. No emotional road map. Just absence. And fear.

I didn't have a framework for mental health back then. I only knew that her leaving left me scared, alone and desperately wanting to *fix* whatever was wrong.

So, I made a silent vow: *If I can just make everything okay at home, maybe she won't get sick again. Maybe she'll stay. Maybe I won't be abandoned.*

I became the good daughter. The peacemaker. The one who kept the house calm, who anticipated her moods, who poured every ounce of herself into making sure Mum was okay. I erased myself to preserve her. I thought if I could create perfect conditions – tidiness, kindness, smiles, calm – then she wouldn't spiral. Then I wouldn't be left.

This is where the seed was planted: *Love means over-functioning. Safety means self-abandonment. Connection means caretaking.*

And while I grew out of that household, the belief came with me.

I didn't play this pattern out in my friendships or in my professional life – there, I held strong boundaries and a strong sense of self, but in intimate relationships, it was different. Romantic love would awaken that old wound – and I'd slip back into the role of the emotional caretaker, the fixer, the one who quietly absorbs and carries.

I found myself choosing men who had suffered trauma – men who, consciously or not, projected the energy of needing to be held, soothed or saved, and I stepped into it. Not because they asked. Not because I didn't know better, but because some part of me still believed that love required it.

I took it all on – their healing, their chaos, their pain – rarely stopping to ask if my own needs were being met. In fact, I'd convinced myself that *helping them* was meeting my needs, because if I could be the one who made a difference, if I could be the one who held it all together, *then maybe I'd finally feel like enough.* That was the quiet trade: their wellbeing for my value.

Over time, the pattern would always unfold the same way: Unequal investment. Unmet needs. Slow-building resentment. And eventually, depletion.

I did this in my marriage. For 14 years, I lived in a continuous loop - giving, managing, holding it all together. Waiting for movement, growth, reciprocity. It didn't come. Not in the way I needed, and by the time I left, I was beyond tired. I was hollowed out by the very caretaking I thought would keep me safe.

But here's the gift: I see it now.

Not with blame. Not with bitterness. But with clarity.

That young girl who tried to save her mother wasn't broken. She was surviving. And the woman who repeated that story in love wasn't weak. She was loyal – to an unconscious contract.

But I'm rewriting/re-*genreing* that contract now. Love no longer means carrying someone else at the cost of myself. It means reciprocity. Wholeness. A meeting, not a rescuing.

And that is the wisdom born of the wound.

Re-genre examples:

Romantic Drama ➔ Sovereignty Story

'I lost myself chasing their love.' → 'I now stand in my own sovereignty, choosing relationships that meet me as an equal and honour my truth.'

Survival ⟶ Rebirth

'I was just getting through each day.' → 'I shed the old skin of survival and stepped into a rebirth – a life of fresh energy and possibility.'

Drama ⟶ Sacred Comedy

'Another cycle of chaos and tears.' → 'Looking back, I can laugh at the absurdity of it all and in choosing peace, I created a new storyline of freedom and joy.'

Romantic Obsession ⟶ Self-Love Story

'I couldn't stop waiting for their message.' → 'I turned that longing inward, discovering the joy of my own company and a love story with myself.'

Tragedy ⟶ Hero's Journey

'My world ended when I lost them.' → 'That heartbreak became the beginning of my hero's journey – the quest that awakened my strength and purpose.'

Sovereignty Takeaway

Your wound was never your weakness. It was your teacher, shaping your becoming. The story was pain—the re-genre is wisdom.

Gentle Reflection: Seeing the Pattern and Re-Genreing the Story

Take a moment to sit quietly. Place a hand on your heart and breathe deeply. Let this become a quiet, honest conversation with your soul.

First, reflect on a repeating pattern in your life that has caused pain. What kinds of situations or relationships tend to loop? What belief might be sitting underneath that pattern? Perhaps it sounds like, 'I'm not enough', or 'I have to earn love', or 'My needs are a burden'. You might write: *I came to believe that...* and complete the sentence with whatever feels most true.

Next, bring to mind a moment when you began to question or outgrow that belief. What shifted for you? What insight, experience or relationship helped you begin to see things differently?

Now, consider what qualities this experience called forth in you. Perhaps it awakened courage, compassion, boundaries or a deeper sense of self-worth. You might name or describe them in your own words.

Then ask yourself how you might now live, love or lead from this wisdom. How has this wound shaped your presence, your purpose, or the way you show up in the world?

Finally, re-genre the story.

Every wound holds a story. But you are not the story, you are the storyteller, the author of your life story.

Finish this sentence:

I am re-genreing my story from [old narrative] to [new one].

For example, from romantic drama to sovereignty story, from fixer fantasy to a path of wholeness, or from tragic worthlessness to soul-led alchemy.

Let it be a sacred declaration, not of who you've been, but of who you're becoming.

You are not defined by what hurt you. You are shaped by how you choose to rise from it. And in that rising, your unique purpose begins to unfold.

This is not the end of your story. It is the beginning of a new chapter, one that you are writing—from a place of wholeness.

What this chapter revealed for you – Use this space to record what resonated, what shifted, what landed.

Chapter 11

You Are the Gift

You are the one you've been waiting for

— Richard Schwartz

(or often attributed to various spiritual traditions)

In the end, this journey has always been about returning. Returning to your own essence. To the part of you that never needed fixing – only remembering.

You are not broken. You were wounded.

And those wounds, when met with love,

become wisdom.

In quantum science, energy is never lost, only transformed. So too with your wounds – nothing is wasted, everything becomes wisdom.

What Healing Really Means (re-genre your story)

Healing is not about erasing what happened. It is about transforming your relationship with it. It is about seeing your pain through the eyes of compassion and recognising that your wounds are not signs of weakness – they are entry points to your deeper self.

A wound is simply a place where life asked you to look more closely. A rupture where your truth was buried beneath survival. Real healing happens when you stop trying to escape the wound and instead, listen to it.

Ask: What was this wound trying to protect me from? What is it asking me to remember?

Healing does not mean the absence of pain. It means you are no longer ruled by it. It means you can hold your past with tenderness and still choose your present with clarity. It's the shift from identifying *as* the wound to living *from* the wisdom it gave you.

And here is the deeper truth: Everything we experience – joy, heartbreak, loss, longing, delight, confusion – every single moment is part of the curriculum of our consciousness. Nothing is wasted. Even the darkest chapters contain a seed of expansion.

The good, the bad, and the painful aren't punishments or mistakes, they are portals. Invitations to rise into new awareness. We do not grow from comfort. We grow when something within us is stretched, questioned or broken open.

Pain is not the opposite of the gift – it *is* the wrapping we must learn to open with tenderness and courage.

Loop Breaking in Action

Every pattern you have untangled, every false belief you've questioned, every emotional spiral you've paused to breathe through—these are signs of healing. This journey has been one of re-claiming, re-membering, and re-turning.

From the belief 'I am not enough' to the truth 'I always was'. From abandonment to self-belonging. From rejection to inner acceptance.

Each experience you've lived was perfectly designed to bring you home to yourself.

Julian, Marcus and Mara

When Mara met Julian, intensity felt like aliveness. He lived in momentum. High stimulation. High attention. A constant appetite for experience. He was wired for thrill, for novelty, for what was bright and slightly out of reach. Women gravitated toward him. He admired beauty openly. Confidence. Boldness. Energy. He was not malicious. He was restless.

Beneath the appetite sat something quieter. A persistent insecurity. A need to feel elevated by what surrounded him. Mara was attractive, capable and composed. He knew he was punching above his weight, and he liked that. When they were out together, he liked what it reflected back to him. She became, subtly, part partner, part proof. Evidence that he was winning. Not because she was deficient, but because he was perpetually reaching. When a man does not feel steady inside himself, he often reaches outward for upgrades. If his world improves, perhaps he improves.

And so, Mara became improvable.

At first it sounded like encouragement. You could take that further. You could push that more. You could do that better. It was not limited to one domain. It was how she dressed, how far she would go sexually, how openly she would experiment, how she parented, how her son should be spoken to, how situations should be handled. There was always a refinement available. A higher level. A better version. What existed was rarely enough for long. Not because it was lacking, but because he was always reaching.

He also had crushes. That was the word he used. Young women who passed through his orbit. One he met up with. One he emailed privately and expressed feelings toward. He told Mara about them almost casually, as though transparency cancelled impact. He never crossed a physical line, but he kept possibility alive. And when a woman lives beside a man who is perpetually scanning, she begins to feel replaceable.

When Mara hesitated, when something did not feel aligned in her body, he did not simply accept it. He challenged it. Her no became a discussion, then a persuasion, then a position to be reconsidered. He would circle back, reframe it, revisit it later, remain with it until her resistance felt harder to sustain than surrender. Sometimes she held her ground. Sometimes the repetition wore her down and she conceded, not from desire but from fatigue. That was the erosion. Not one disagreement, but the accumulation. The subtle positioning of her as both project and trophy.

When she tried to name the pattern, he listened. Then he persisted. Not because he misunderstood her, but because his needs were primary. If something increased stimulation or status, it outweighed her discomfort. Her boundaries became obstacles to negotiate around rather than limits to honour. She was not being met. She was being managed. So she stopped negotiating. She ended the relationship. Three years.

After Julian came Marcus. Where Julian evaluated, Marcus affirmed. Constant admiration. No suggestions. No correction. No scanning. You are perfect. You do not need to change a thing. I have never met anyone like you. For a woman who had felt evaluated, refined and replaceable, this felt like relief. Safety. Rest.

Pain, especially when followed quickly by comfort, creates pendulums. When we have felt improved, we gravitate toward unconditional acceptance. When we have felt replaceable, we choose someone who makes us feel irreplaceable. Mara swung from calibration to reassurance, from being a project to being adored. She stayed with Marcus for fourteen years, long enough to discover that constant praise can also conceal truth, that reassurance without transparency can destabilise just as deeply as correction without containment.

Years later, after her relationship with Marcus ended, Julian reappeared. Time had softened him. The overt intensity was lower. But the core wiring remained. The instinct to position himself above. The reflex to correct. The quiet need to diminish what unsettled his own sense of adequacy. And the familiar narration returned. Who was beautiful. Who stood out. Who caught his eye. What he found attractive. And how she could adjust herself to meet that standard. Not as suggestion but as expectation. The form had changed. The orientation had not.

Life does not always send a new teacher. Sometimes it sends the same one to see if the lesson has integrated.

This time she did not need years. She did not need evidence. She did not need to doubt her perception. She recognised the pattern. She calmly told him they were relationally incompatible. Fifteen weeks. That was the evidence. Not because the attraction was gone. Not because she was immune. But because awareness moved faster than conditioning.

Conditioning does not disappear. It checks whether it still has access. The same personality may return. The same attraction may spark. The same dynamic may test the edges. Integration reveals itself in duration reduction.

Three years.

Fourteen years.

Fifteen weeks.

Awareness does not erase conditioning. It shortens its lifespan.

After pain, we often overcorrect. We swing from evaluation to reassurance, from improvement to protection. Pendulums feel like progress because they move. But integration is not the swing. It is the steady centre. Mara no longer becomes a project. She no longer becomes proof. She no longer confuses validation with value. She meets herself first. And when patterns quietly ask, Do I still have access? She answers with action. She leaves sooner.

Sovereignty Takeaway

Every wound brought you closer to yourself. Every pattern carried a seed of wisdom. The story was striving, the re-genre is remembering you are the gift.

Gentle Reflection: Witnessing the Shift

Take a quiet moment. Breathe deeply. Let this practice be a sacred conversation between your past and present self.

Begin by writing a letter from the part of you that once believed, 'I am not enough'. What did this part believe about the world, about love, about your place in it? What did it need that it didn't receive? What has it taught you through its pain?

Now, write a response from your present self. This version of you holds wisdom, clarity and compassion. What do you now know that the younger you didn't? How can you hold this part with love, without trying to fix it?

Finally, complete this sentence with your own truth:

'I no longer ____.

I now choose ____.'

For example: 'I no longer abandon myself to be chosen. I choose myself first.' Or 'I no longer shrink to stay safe. I honour my fullness.'

Let this truth guide how you show up, how you speak to yourself, how you choose relationships and how you create your future.

Let your life become the embodiment of your healing. Let your worth be non-negotiable. Let your presence be the gift.

You are already enough. You always were. And the world is better because you are in it.

What this chapter revealed for you – Use this space to record what resonated, what shifted, what landed.

You don't wait for a new life.

You become it.

If you're ready to keep stepping into that version of you: www.marniesole.com

Acknowledgements

To Louie,

My ever-evolving son – steady, curious and generous. Thank you for choosing me. Your presence called me into deeper love, truth and accountability. You are my greatest teacher, my mirror and my joy.

In this season of my life – the crone years of this timeline – I see with unmistakable clarity that the greatest reward for all the inner work I've done is *you*. Not in theory. Not in words. But in *witnessing* – watching the way you move through the world with curiosity, integrity and self-inquiry. Watching you do the work.

You are a sensational human. Watching how people light up in your presence – how they feel seen, valued and safe around you, is its own kind of medicine. Your humour, your care, your generosity… they are evidence of what becomes possible when we choose to turn inward and transform.

You are the living proof of why this work matters. You are the ancestral legacy, walking. And long after I leave this earth, I will watch from above – smiling as your children, and their children, continue to benefit from the path you've chosen, and the path I cleared. This is the legacy.

To Carol and Pete,

My real, raw, *funny-as-fuck*, half-sister and half-brother. Fun. Irreverent. Brilliant in ways the mainstream could never define – and wouldn't know what to do with even if it tried.

We shared a father – though he was barely in your lives and only marginally more in mine. His legacy wasn't presence, but absence. Abandonment, and yet somehow, through that absence, something powerful emerged.

When we reconnected nearly 20 years ago, we picked up threads that were barely there in childhood and wove them into something rich and real. What started as reconnection became recognition – of shared wounds, shared resilience and a shared ability to turn pain into something far more interesting.

What still blows me away is how you've both taken your lives – the chaos, the trauma, the absurdity – and turned them into wildly successful, uniquely defined versions of a good life. We live lives that are gloriously offbeat, wonderfully non-conforming, and none of us fit the mould. Thank God.

We each carry stories of homelessness, abuse, heartbreak and sheer madness – and somehow, we've found the humour in it all. You never let the story own you. You flipped it. You shaped it. You made it your own. Even now, when you tease me about being the one who 'got the pony', I love it, because inside that humour is healing – the best kind. The kind that doesn't take itself too seriously or render us victims.

Therapists might help people unpack their pain, but they never ask: What if your story doesn't need to be rewritten – just re-genred? What if it's not a tragedy, but a dark comedy with a twist of soul? What if you rewrote the story as a comedy, not a tragedy? What if laughing *with* the pain was the medicine?

You two are my muses in that way. Living proof that laughter is a portal. That irreverence is a kind of wisdom, and that even the worst stories can shine when told with grit, guts and a little madness.

I can't wait for the next time we sit down again and mine our lives for gold ….and laugh our brains out.

www.ingramcontent.com/pod-product-compliance
Lightning Source LLC
Chambersburg PA
CBHW070519140726
48132CB00030B/417

* 9 7 8 1 7 6 4 5 9 7 5 0 0 *